Reflections In the Sand

Author- Anna Maria Fierro- Fasciana

Cover Design- Gaetano Luca Fasciana- Photography

All Rights Reserved

Quotes from _Reflections in the Sand_

As humans we all share the same fundamental needs for love and acceptance. *(First in my Life, page 16).*

It is my belief that without some form of spiritual awareness we tend to walk this Earth feeling like lonely, secluded individuals. *(First in my Life, page 16).*

It is by this process that self esteem, self love and self acceptance are woven together, generating a sense of security and belonging and being in 'sync' with the Universe. *(In Sync with the Universe, page 20).*

I believe that it is those children who have developed a well balanced life that realize their magnificence and are able to ride the waves towards excellence. *(In Sync with the Universe, page 20).*

The journey is God's gift to us the choice to participate is ours. *(Relinquishing the Blame, page 36).*

Changes in our lives are essential. Like the eternal wheel, nothing remains the same and everything comes full circle. *(Coming Full Circle, page 13).*

Then, for the sake of who we are, we learn to love ourselves. *(Resisting Compromise, page 38).*

It is my belief that we came into this world with an agenda, to learn about and experience various aspects of life, fragrance and thorns included. *(Mixed Blessings, page 29).*

It is when we realize that we have options that we are able to look through the walls of fear and see the love that glows brightly beyond. *(Inspired by Love, page 23).*

Faith has been known to move mountains. Therefore, it only stands to reason that faith, and of course love, make the world go round. *(Inspired By Love, page 23).*

Remembering that it matters not which road ones takes, for every road leads back to our soul. *(In the Beginning, page 22).*

It is when we make the time to look within ourselves that we can get lost and find ourselves *(Seek and you shall Find, page 40).*

I believe that life is a continual test of endurance, while we may often stumble and fall, we get back up and continue on.
(Endurance, page 14).

Follow your heart and never give up. Never give up on you! *(Never Give Up, page 31).*

The acceptance of self is probably the greatest gift that any person could ever give to oneself. For acceptance, embraced by self, equals pure love. *(Acceptance of Self, page 8).*

As a spiritual people, our principal concern ought to contain one very important ingredient, that of being real, being true to oneself.
(Colour me Real, page 11).

I hunger for that which completes me and allows for me to feel whole.
(Our Soul, page 32).

It is only then that we are ready to embrace the knowledge that we are all one and the same with the Universe.
(The Many Faces of Fear, page 44).

Index

1. A Collection of Pearls
2. A Hero Within
3. *The Art of Life*
4. A Moment in Time
5. A Passage of Time
6. *Awareness*
7. A Passion for Life
8. Acceptance of Self
9. *Always Me*
10. An Illusion Called Fear
11. Colour Me Real
12. *This Moment*
13. Coming Full Circle
14. Endurance
15. *Being True to Yourself*
16. First In My Life
17. *Autumn*
18. Forgiveness
19. *God's Creations*
20. In Sync with The Universe
21. *Alone*
22. In The Beginning
23. Inspired By Love
24. *My Soul*
25. Life on the Merry-Go-Round
26. Looking at Life

27. *Time To Ponder*
28. Miracles
29. Mixed Blessings
30. *A Different Path*
31. Never Give Up
32. Our Soul
33. *Saying Goodbye*
34. Releasing the Past
35. *I Am*
36. Relinquishing the Blame
37. *Tall green Grass*
38. Resisting Compromise
39. *Mr. X*
40. Seek and You Shall Find
41. *Planet Earth*
42. Sitting in Judgment
43. *Trusting the Lord*
44. The Many Faces of Fear
45. *The Storm*
46. The Wave Makers
47. *On a Clear Day*
48. Two sides of the Same Coin
49. *My Home/My Haven*
50. Fresh White Snow
51. *Fleeting*

A Collection of Pearls

I collect only pearls.

Many friends have come into my life over the years. Yet it never ceases to amaze me how friendships are born, nurtured and quite often let go only to turn around and begin the process many times over.

Of course there have also been times in my life where I have had to grieve the loss of certain relationships. Even so I have discovered that there is light at the end of the tunnel and that the rewards have far outweighed any losses that life has thrown my way.

I do not believe in things happening by mere chance rather I believe that the Universe brings people together at different times in their lives so that all might serve in being present for one another and in providing stepping stones for spiritual growth.

I have learned never to look at any relationship with anything other than the utmost of respect. I believe that my life is far richer today thanks also to each of those individuals who shared a part of their life with me.

For me, friendships are an integral part of my life and by cultivating them with an extra measure of love, I am certain to harvest only pearls.

A Hero Within

It has been said that within each human lies a potential hero.

These words alone have been just enough information to have aroused a sense of curiosity within me. Curiosity, that once fuelled, would turn itself into a much deeper desire for further knowledge and growth, which has by far turned out to be my greatest quest.

The ultimate quest, of course, is to allow the hero to emerge from within. What I have come to realize is that the only way to achieve this task is to delve wholeheartedly into the very depths of my soul, in search of my true self. Which also translates into bringing forth every tiny fibre of emotional pain that I have ever tucked away, because of my fears. Now to be relived, experienced and finally having the courage to face those fears that have held me in bondage for ever so long. It is by facing these fears that yet another level of consciousness is able to be reached.

I am making my choice in life, by participating in the ultimate experience of life and I am reclaiming the hero within me...

The Art of Life

Life is art
in action and
I am here
to blend in
my colours
In my own unique way
I too share in
the weaving
of the
tapestry of life
As the story
itself unfolds
a bittersweet feeling
reaches out and
envelops my soul
With this revelation
comes a whole new direction
As I continue weaving
the threads
of my own destiny
it becomes more apparent
where life
is leading me
Life is art
in action and
I am here
to blend in
my
colours...

A Moment in Time

Life is a gift that should never be taken for granted nor wasted. Yet many of us often live life as though we were immortal.

How many of us believe that everything can wait often saying "there is always tomorrow"?

At times even putting off speaking to those closest to us whether through pride, stubbornness or just through plain ignorance. Then a tragedy strikes and the moment that might have been becomes lost to us forever.

I am certain that many of us can attest to having, at one time or another, experienced something along those lines. Quite often, even followed by a deep sense of regret, through choices that we had made earlier on, leaving us unable to find solace within ourselves.

A whole lifetime spent on this earth making memories. Some of which will be cherished, some we may wish could be changed, while some others we would rather forget. Consequently, all of those memories we ourselves had a hand in creating. Memories, now belonging to each and every one of us.

Someone who had lived a very long life had once been asked, as she stood pensively by her window, "What have you learned from life?" Turning, she clearly spoke these words to the young person asking, **"La vita e, una facciata di finestra."/ "Life is like a quick glance through a window, which is over in the blink of an eye."**

I believe that statement says it all for Life is but a mere moment in time and if we are not living through awareness it will forever be lost to us...

A Passage of Time

It may appear that, no matter how one looks at it, life seems to be all about losses, while failing to notice the positives as we continually focus on the negative.

How many of us stand back to look at our own lives and observe how many different types of losses we have personally suffered over the years? Such as the loss of a job, a loved one, a friend, a relationship, our youth and the list goes on...

In life there are certainly no guarantees. That lesson is demonstrated to us, each and every day, through one form or another.

During the time of my childhood, my adolescence and in being a young woman, there were times when I too had dreamed of what my life might have been. Sadly, I unknowingly cheated myself of my dreams by living my life for others as though I had more than one life to live.

Today I have come to believe that there is a positive side to each one of our losses. Through the pain of loss one can experience spiritual growth, gain wisdom, knowledge and know what real joy truly means. Quite often it is because of it that we learn to truly appreciate moments of laughter, of sharing and caring for others.

I believe that rather than focussing on life as being merely about losses, we would do well to periodically examine our gains. Remembering too that life is made up of moments, yes only moments that, unless we are truly present, can become lost thus passing us by unnoticed.

Life's precious moments, in all of its' magic, has the eternal capacity of making the difference in the quality of each one of our lives.

Awareness

Becoming aware of my life
to the way things are
Accepting and forgiving
of the things I am not
Acknowledging my feelings
which I chose to ignore
Travelling in time
to moments gone by
Releasing the hurt
before saying
goodbye...

A Passion for Life

There is a time to be born and a time to die but more importantly there is a time to live. To live life as though each breath we inhale were to be our last.

How many times have we heard the expression "as though each day were to be our last?" How much importance does each one of us place on this statement? How often do we tend to take our lives for granted?

No one is guaranteed their next moment, let alone a tomorrow. We have the *present,* a word, within itself, that tells us it is a gift and that our life is the Now. All that is certain is that only *this* moment matters.

One of the most important things which we continually ignore, is the child within us. That part of us that keeps us connected to our spirit, to the sense of what life is about. Have you ever noticed children at play? They have fun, laugh and say openly what they think and feel without reservation, without thinking of the repercussions. When was the last time you ever felt freedom?

Looking back at life, was there ever a time in your youth that you can recall spending days just having fun, if only just in fantasizing about your future, *sognando ad occhi apperti, or in daydreaming with your eyes wide open.* Perhaps planning and even hoping to change the world into something better? The answers to our questions lays deep within each person. Answers kept safe, within a sacred space, that we ourselves have the freedom to access.

If we choose to embrace anything at all then let it be the full experience of living life.

Acceptance of Self

Searching outwardly for acceptance seems to be the theme, for many people...

As I ponder upon my own life, I realize that I too have spent a great deal of time looking to others for acceptance, for a place of belonging and for the need to be loved. All of which came to me at a very high cost.

Life has taught me that by looking to others for acceptance I dilute the essence of my own existence. If acceptance is required to avoid this, then my lesson becomes one of learning how to accept myself, for exactly who I am, without any reservation and by developing a clear understanding that the only person whose opinion really matters in my own life is mine. Feeling good about myself can only serve in the unconditional acceptance of everyone else in my life too.

I once heard said that "the answers we seek lay within us." I must admit that, at the time, it all sounded quite abstract to me. Today, however, I can safely say that it only stands to reason that when the search is turned inward, instead of directed to outward influences, the answers seem to gently rise to the surface, like pouring oil on troubled waters.

The acceptance of self is probably the greatest gift that any person could give to oneself. For acceptance, embraced by self, equals pure love.

Always Me

To know life is to know feelings
and yet I run as far as I can
for fear of what I may see
Driven by fear away from myself
away from the friend that
lays within me
The friend that patiently waits
for me to return
I return to my feelings only
to see
that inside of myself
there's a me

An Illusion Called Fear

Have you ever wondered what life would be like if unfounded fear could be released?

At times it is as though fear envelops us in such a way that life itself feels virtually impossible to go on with.

At times fear can come to us as a warning signal against possible danger while, in other instances, it can be very debilitating and destructive. It can also create havoc by compelling us to erect emotional barriers for protection against the unknown.

I remember a time in my youth when I felt fear at the mere mention of the word "death". After all, death meant the end of life as we know it "the dark unknown!" I later came to realize that it had not been so much about death that I feared, as it was about the fear of living!

Like so many others, I learned at a very tender age that life meant hurt, pain and suffering. After which my mind continually reinforced that belief each time something went wrong in my life.

My quest for the truth, of my own reality, has provided me with a greater insight and awareness, not only of myself but also of the illusionary fear that had taken root within my imagination.

I can either choose to look into the face of fear, feel the pain and move forward with life.

Or choose to just simply give into the fear, continue being overwhelmed and remain stuck. Only to watch life, pass me by...

As for me, I chose to move forward, **with life!**

Colour Me Real

Why is it that so many of us seem to focus only on the unhappy events that have occurred in our lives? Why do we cling to memories that have caused us such emotional pain?

Have we become such creatures of habit that we dare not even remember how to feel? Do we question ourselves as to the purpose of having emotional pain in our lives?

Have we become so detached from our feelings that we would rather believe that the concept of pain is but a curse upon us? Do we really hold a belief system based solely on fear?

Emotional pain ought to be viewed, simply, as blessings in disguise. They are opportunities that life offers us, in order to help us grow spiritually. It is up to us to recognize them as such so that we may aspire to still greater challenges.

As a spiritual people, our principal concern ought to contain one very important ingredient, that of being real, being true to oneself. When we make time to learn about and acknowledge our feelings, we are helping ourselves by creating an understanding and developing a deeper sense of self awareness.

It is in the blessing of people and events, that helps us feel pain, that we are able to get closure for those hurtful feelings, which allow us to make peace with the past. If we leave the colours of negative emotions out of the picture, our portrait remains incomplete.

So please, colour me real...

This Moment

At this very moment
I am alive
I am breathing
talking
and I am thinking
This precious moment
shall I savour
as one would
a drop of water
in the midst of
a desert sand
This moment
I shall treasure
for never will I relive
this moment
again

Coming Full Circle

Life is an eternally spinning wheel which brings continual change but always comes around full circle to complete its' cycle.

As a spiritual people, we came into this world with an awareness of who we were and constantly evolved by gathering knowledge from the lessons we each had chosen to learn.

At birth we all received the same spiritual gift, that of having a *free will*. Freedom to make our own choices in life. An ability to make choices powerful enough to serve in mapping out the course of our lives. A gift that has become for us the instrument that determines our destiny.

In short, there are no coincidences in life. Whatever takes place in it, does not just simply happen. They are a combination of circumstances which we helped bring about by the choices we made.

When it comes to people and relationships, we attract into our lives those through whom our greatest lessons can be learned. Even though things go awry and our personal lives may suffer turbulence, we need to remember that *we* are instrumental in creating these stressful circumstances for a reason; to experience lessons in order to cultivate our spiritual growth.

Changes in our lives are essential. Like the eternal wheel nothing remains the same and yet everything comes full circle.

Endurance

Failure is not in falling down it is in not wanting to try and get back up.

Unfortunately, struggles are a fact of life. For some the struggles are often greater. But each of us have our own cross to bare.

With that said, it would appear that each time something goes wrong in our lives something very right seems to follow.

I can recall certain events in my own life when I felt as though my own world had come to an end only to later realize how truly blessed I really was.

It is only through personal trials and suffering that we allow ourselves to grow. For how are we to know real happiness if we have never experienced sadness?

It is through personal growth that we learn to live without regrets. Then we are able to look at our lives and the people who have passed through it as genuine treasures, from which we have learned and fortunately grown.

I believe that life is a continual test of endurance. While we may often stumble and fall, we get back up and continue on...

Being True To Yourself

Speak freely of
your feelings
do not hold them inside
for as long as you do
you play the game
you wear the mask
you are not yourself
Listen carefully
to your heart and
your instincts
for they tell you
no lies
If it doesn't feel good inside
you know that
it's not right
Speak freely of
your feelings
reach out and claim
your higher self
Speak freely
your feelings
and follow your own
path...

First In My Life

Suppose that in the eyes of The Creator each one of us is the centre of our Universe and that the love and happiness we need does not have to come from outside forces. Perhaps it never has. Can we generate our own love by how we value ourselves? Does the love we receive from others serve to enhance what we already feel?

Truth has it that each one of us must come first for ourselves, in order to be a whole healthy human being. After all, is it not when we feel good about ourselves that we are able to share our love with someone else?

There are many ways in which to express the message of self love and probably one of the most appropriate was told me by someone very dear to me, "The best thing you can do for me, is to take care of you." The simplicity of that statement is truly an open expression of love.

As humans, we all share the same fundamental needs for love and acceptance. Unfortunately for us, however, somewhere along life's path we learned to look to others to satisfy these needs. Only we can fulfill this task by accepting and loving ourselves for who we are, first and foremost. It is only when we fully accept ourselves that we can make a significant difference in our own lives and in the lives of those around us.

It is my belief that, without some form of spiritual awareness, we tend to walk this earth feeling like lonely, secluded individuals, not realizing the power and love that was given to us at the moment of our creation.

Autumn

Autumn arrives
spreading it's rich colours
all around
leaves gently float
and find their way to the ground
to cover the earth
with a magical quilt
a patchwork
of brightly coloured leaves
laid out softly upon the ground
Then a gust of wind
A thousand leaves
scatter...

Forgiveness

"Forgiveness is in remembering how human we all are. In forgiving, we acknowledge our own human weaknesses."

How often do circumstances arise in our lives when we feel hurt by someone's insensitivity? Possibly even resenting and holding grudges against them for months or even years at a time?

Why is it that humankind has not yet figured out a way in which to accept all others as being equals, in creativity, in spirit and in mortality? Do we not all have the same needs and wants as human beings?

Quite often we are our own worst enemies, for there are times when we find it difficult if not impossible to forgive and then to stop berating our own selves.

How many of us tend to use that emotional whip to lash out at ourselves anytime things do not work out for us, while further hurling statements of inadequacies upon our own selves?

I have spent the better part of my life trying to please and to prove to others that I was good enough, only to later realize that I gave others more value than I ever gave myself. I have had to forgive myself for not thinking myself worthy.

A very dear friend once said, "If you hold on to the past with both hands, you will have no hand to reach out to the future."

Let go, let God--- Forgive, and you shall be forgiven.

God's Creations

Where have I been
all of my life
not to have noticed
that time is required for me
Time to ponder
on what life is about
time taken
to listen to the birds
singing ever so passionately
high above the trees
The Lord made a world
then filled it with
sweet splendour
for you and for me
for the whole world
to see
All we need to do
is allow ourselves the time
to set our minds
free

In Sync With The Universe

As caregivers our primary concern ought to be that of helping our children develop a well balanced life, while we continue to strive for balance within ourselves.

For me this task required getting in touch with feelings that governed the way in which I perceived life. This meant that I had to discover new ways to allow for more faith and trust in myself.

By looking at it from a child's perspective, I can say that it comes down to a question of trust. That is, a child's trusting in their very existence in those people in whose care they have been placed.

The position of caregiver is by no means a small task. It comes with a major responsibility, consisting of hard work, dedication, patience, sacrifice, selflessness and probably the most important of all, an abundant supply of unconditional love.

It means taking on the responsibility to provide children with a loving, nurturing environment, whereby they can be heard, respected and trusted. In essence, it means providing an environment which makes it possible for children to reach within their very soul and learn to trust their own instincts.

It is by this process that self esteem, self love and self acceptance are woven together, in turn generating a sense of security and belonging as well as a feeling within the individual of being in sync with the Universe.

I believe that it is those children who have developed a well balanced life that realize their magnificence and are able to ride the waves towards excellence.

Alone

I feared the thought
of being alone
once I had you and
I still felt alone
alone is just
a state of mind
for in reality
every human that walks the earth
stands alone
alone is just
a state of mind
for now that I have found myself
I no longer
feel
alone

In The Beginning

We have all heard the famous saying "All roads lead to Rome!"

I feel the same holds true where our souls are considered. I believe that from the moment we are born, we are truly unique beings in every respect. God really knew what he was doing when He created humankind. Creating each of us whole in every sense of the word.

I believe life begins within our very hearts and soul and in knowing that it is God's, Holy Spirit, that lives within the very centre of our being.

As infants and young children we tend to move away from our souls by slowly integrating into society. While in that process we are forgetting our primal existence our specialness and more commonly distancing ourselves from God.

While speaking on my own behalf, this is how I view life today. Having had my own share of bittersweet experiences, I have also had the good fortune of rediscovering a part of me that I too had lost long ago. The part that connected me to God, to my soul...

I believe that in order to find oneself and restore the happiness lost to us at the time of our birth one must return to the core of ones' own being.

Remembering that it matters not which road one takes for.... every road leads us back to our soul...

Inspired by Love

It has been said that love makes the world go round.

If this statement wasn't true, then what purpose would it serve for us in being here? What significance would our lives have if they were bereft of love?

Love is an inner barometer with which we are able to make sense of our lives. It is an essence that gives us balance, hope, inspiration and bestows harmony to our spirits.

Yet it is not in receiving love but rather in the giving of ourselves, for the betterment of others, that helps promote our own inner healing.

We must also realize that before we can love others in full measure, we must be able to love ourselves equally. To get through the dilemma of receiving love from ourselves unconditionally and not because we serve others like some sort of trade. We must be willing to look within and determine if we come from a place of love or a place of need.

Recognizing the neediness within us, is our souls' way of providing an instinctual warning of where our vulnerabilities lie. It is through awareness of our weaknesses that we then can begin to make a difference for ourselves.

Awareness in any situation becomes a tool. After all it is when we realize that we have options that we are able to look through the walls of fear and see the love that glows brightly beyond.

It will be through the choices that we make that will determine if we are to settle for crumbs or help ourselves to the whole loaf.

My Soul

There is a place
deep within my heart
a place that
only I can visit
A place from whence God
beckons to me
softly saying
come and visit me
come and lean on me
let me be
your foundation
let me be
your place of repose
look to me
for whatever you need
for I am your salvation
I am the comforter of
your soul

Life On The Merry-Go-Round

At times life seems like a merry-go-round which continually spins round and round. Where once in a while fortunate ones are strewn to the ground, slowly picking themselves up, with questioning eyes looking back at the merry-go-round.

It would appear that from the time we are born, until such time that we are laid to rest many of us live out our lives in fear. We learn very early on that life is not a safe place and that it takes far more courage to live than to die.

Fear often comes to us in various wrappings in numerous ways depths and magnitudes. As we become more conscious of our feelings we also become more aware of how we tend to shrink from them. Avoidance of our feelings at all costs is a learned skill used to avoid the painful content of our emotions.

While together we all make up a Universal family, we journey the path of life alone. Often the mere thought of being alone fills us with terror, prompting us to latch on to others and objects in order to give us the feeling of safety all the while avoiding the real issue.

It is only when we acknowledge our fear and allow ourselves permission to experience whatever we are feeling that makes life by far easier in helping to find solace within ourselves.

Life is also a magnificent merry-go-round and we have been invited to participate in all that it has to offer be it good or bad.

Let us not be afraid to live life let us instead rejoice in being alive. As always the choice remains our own.

Looking at Life

Life itself is a journey, a continuous journey that comes to an end only when life itself extinguishes.

How often do we find ourselves wishing for things to happen, as in looking forward to a trip, anxious to arrive at a destination, spending time with people whom we want to be with and so on?

Quite often, life itself seems to pass us by and, before we know it, months or even years have slipped away unnoticed, right in front of our very eyes. We then, surprised, find ourselves asking, "where did the time go to?"

This journey that we are on, could be considered like a train ride. We board at one station and eagerly await departure, then we begin counting the seconds before we reach our destination. So caught up are we, in the time taking, that we are unable to enjoy or even acknowledge the beautiful view, as life itself often passes us by, unnoticed.

Life is so precious. Yet many of us are so busy looking forward to seeing the yield we finally harvest from our labours that we forget to look at the things in life that really matter. Too little time is spent on those things that make us smile and bring us joy. It takes all of these little things in life to make up the bigger picture.

We all, at one time or another, have our moments of tears of laughter and moments that we would rather forget. The important thing is to live and experience every moment, be it positive or negative.

For in the end, all these moments put together, will tell the story, of our lives and of who we are.

Time To Ponder

Sitting on a rock
by the edge of the water
looking out as far as the eye
can see
Sailboats floating by
on the surface
of a glassy sea
Thoughts fill my mind
as the boats drift by
wondering where life
is taking me
A new path
another journey
more life to explore
Like the sun that sets
in the eve
we are always in search
of more...

Miracles

I believe in Miracles!

Have you ever found yourself in a situation whereby the only thing you had left was prayer?

At certain times situations arise in life wherein we have no control over the events that take place. In prayer, however, we do have choices. We can either choose to pray choose to believe or we can choose to do nothing.

Faith is something found deep within our hearts within our very soul. It is the belief that God lives within us regardless of race, colour or creed. Faith is not reserved for a mere handful of individuals but meant for us all.

It wasn't until just recently that I fully understood the power in faith, belief and prayer. It was only recently that I truly realized that God not only exists but speaks to us when we call upon Him and are ready to listen to His words.

Each one of us is special in the eyes of God. Each of us is like a precious jewel to Him. He asks only for our love and in return rewards us with many special gifts.

In a recent conversation with God, I discovered that He also has a great sense of humour for in the midst of our conversation, after I had asked God for a miracle, He turned and said, "It took a miracle to get us talking."

To all that has taken place in my life, I can only add that my cup runneth over. I have been blessed, I received my miracle and I have God within me.

Mixed Blessings

"I have been collecting nothing but scars all of my life."

These were the words that a very dear friend uttered in a softly spoken, heart wrenching voice as she sat pensively and recalled to mind certain events from long ago that, even to this day, have the power to stir deep emotions within her.

I have no doubt whatsoever that many of us are able to relate to that statement. Some of us have even lived through situations which we considered to be our own personal inferno.

What I have come to understand from all of this is that if our outlook on life is based on one of judgement, then whenever painful situations arise we are more apt to view our lives as a personal hell, rather than recognizing these situations as gifts or opportunities for spiritual growth.

My belief is that we came into this world with an agenda; to learn about and experience various aspects of life, fragrance and thorns included. At some point during the course of time we developed a notion that life should be lived in a fairy tale "happily ever after" fashion. An ideal that to this day remains a fallacy, leaving many individuals totally perplexed in its' wake.

Life is about taking comfort in the knowledge that all is well and that everything that happens in our lives happens for the right reasons.

Life is about having faith and accepting it's joy and sorrow without measuring, as God's hand slowly but gently sifts through the chaff and grain of our lives.

A Different Path

I have chosen a path
different from yours
the path I took
may not have been the one
of your choice
and though at times
we fail to agree
I know that where I am
I need to be
and even though it was
not your choice
try to remember that
it is my life
my journey
my choice

Never Give Up

The easiest thing to do in life is to give up. Anyone of us can do that and with very little effort, I might add.

It would appear that life itself is one big struggle and that the effort required on our part alone just to survive often becomes more than any one human being can even bear.

With that said how many of us really fight for what we want? How many of us even think that *we* are worth it? How many of us continue standing up for what we need, for as long as we can draw breath?

Recently I had been described by a close friend saying "you are a very resilient woman, considering your own life experience." Looking back at my life I must admit that I too am surprised that I didn't crack under the pressure and abuse that I survived for many years.

All along I had thought that I was a weak person. Now I have come to realize that only the strong could have endured what I lived through.

I believe my tenacity has a lot to do with who I am. It often compels me to do things all the way or not at all. I feel the same holds true even when it comes to my friends and or relationships.

Hope is said to be the last thing to die. So as long as there is life there is hope. With that in mind I shall continue my quest into acquiring that of which my heart and my life shall need.

Follow your heart and never give up hope. Never give up on you!

Our Soul

One of the biggest and most important adventures of our lives takes place when we finally discover and acknowledge our soul.

While many people may refer to the soul by various other names such as the super ego, higher self, subconscious, spirit and so on my belief is that we all nonetheless possess a soul.

I also believe that the discovery of our soul can only take place if we choose to embark on the journey of wanting to know who we truly are. That is to say not as someone's child, sibling, spouse, or parent, but rather as knowing the very essence that dwells deep within each and every one of us.

It has been through my own personal experience of grief and loss that I have, on numerous occasions, experienced states of unimaginable emotional pain. Of course without these experiences emotional growth would have been impossible to reach. For history itself has proven that one must experience pain in order to grow both emotionally and spiritually.

Emotional growth and self-discovery is a lifelong journey. While this part of my journey has been gratifying, I have also come to realize that within each fibre of my being I sense there is something greater yet that remains to be unearthed. Far more than the eye can see, I feel that in order to be complete something more is required of me.

I have been on a journey in search of the being that lays within me. Having travelled this far I further wish to explore the something more. I choose to know intimately that part of me called a soul.

I hunger for that which completes me and allows me to feel whole...

Saying Goodbye

Looking back at years gone by
childhood memories
often make it difficult
to say good-bye
as I continue upon my path
I am giving my life another chance
and
though the past
remains
the same
I know tomorrow
shall bring me
change

Releasing the Past

When we hold on to the past with both hands we leave no hand free to reach out to the future.

How often have we found ourselves in an emotional struggle because of past experiences or have allowed the past to hold on to us emotionally?

Oddly enough this phenomenon seems to occur most frequently when we live our lives in a state of fear or guilt. Those two feelings often make it difficult for us to let go.

Fear and guilt are learned traits. Some people have been raised to simply experience life, while many others have been raised to believe that one either obeys the rules without question or risks emotional pain by being considered bad when making a so-called mistake.

I believe that when we choose to experience life we are helping ourselves by promoting our natural expression of self. After all is it not through experience that we are able to learn?

Through these experiences we can learn to accept ourselves and set forth the necessary conditions for spiritual growth. These same conditions allow us to move forward while gently embracing maturity as we take part in evolving from childhood into adulthood.

Only then are we truly able to loosen our grip and let go of the past.

I Am

To whom does it matter
What colour
I am
What importance does it have
where I come from
The language I speak is of
no consequence
I exist upon
this earth
Through the grace of God
and I live
in
His Universe

Relinquishing The Blame

Has there ever been a time in your life when you found yourself in an emotional crisis, blaming someone else for whatever difficulties you may have been experiencing?

We, as children, learned not only to look outside of ourselves to find answers to our questions as a means to fulfill our needs, we also learned how to lay blame of our unfulfilled expectations on those around us.

This resentment is born out of misinformation, keeping us unaware that no other human being has any power over us unless, we give them the power. No one can hurt us emotionally. We do that ourselves by diminishing our self worth after failing to meet unattainable expectations of ourselves.

The only apparent solution in changing this vicious cycle named blame, is for us to assume full responsibility for our own lives, our own actions and our own pain. In doing so, we would not only achieve emotional healing, but would also make it possible for ourselves to embark on the greatest journey that ever was.

This journey could take us far and beyond the realm of imagination, to the very depths of our soul, where we can rediscover the very essence of who we are, our connection to one another and the purpose for our being on this earth.

From this place, we could then exercise our abilities to relinquish blame, to forgive, to accept ourselves and to love who we are then relish in the freedom that it brings us.

The journey is God's gift to us the choice to participate is ours.

Tall Green Grass

To a meadow
of tall green grass
I am being drawn
to come and lay
within it's clasp
as a soft wind blows
gently finding it's way
amongst each blade of grass
I feel the comfort and
the closeness of The Lord
as I lay here
within the beauty
of this
tall green grass

Resisting Compromise

Compromising who we are seems to be the general concession for many individuals when the desire for love turns into a need.

Ah, yes love. An all-encompassing feeling that not only can empower us by providing meaning and purpose to our existence, but can also in a mere heartbeat use its' capacity to turn our emotions completely upside down...

For some people the fear of aloneness is enough to create within them an overwhelming state of anxiety. This in turn puts into motion feelings of helplessness and unworthiness. Given that emotional frame of mind they can actually convince themselves that their lives would be totally meaningless unless they are able to share it with that other someone regardless of the status of the relationship.

Sadly to say that anytime we become fear driven regardless of the situation or relationship we place ourselves in a vulnerable state. Whereby we risk surrendering the most precious gift that we hold in our possession - our own identity.

Whether we choose to believe it or not the love we are in search of cannot be given to us by someone else. That love does exist but only within ourselves. It is we who hold it captive and the only way of releasing it is by facing the very fears that prevent us from looking within in order for us to feel it.

Then for the sake of who we are we learn to love ourselves.

Mr. X

Only when you've gone hungry
can you know how I feel
standing in a lineup
with hands held out before me
in a strange place
where no one comes to know my name
made to feel less
than the man that I am
standing here before you
dejected and disempowered
to whom do I turn
when you turn me down
only when you stand here
as I do
will the thought
even hit you
as to the human
that I am
for I am you
and you are me
and what connects us
is our
humanity

Seek and You Shall Find

The more you lose yourself, the more you find yourself.

For some of us, there comes a time in our lives when we are brought down to our knees. Only then, do we even begin to realize just how lost we have felt for the better part of our lives.

Until such time as this happens, we often go through life as though being on automatic pilot existing solely by going through the motions of being physically present. While in reality, keeping ourselves from participating in life emotionally.

While under these particular circumstances, life seems to pass us by unnoticed. For subconsciously we have chosen to become the observer rather than feeling and participating in whatever experiences that life is continually unfolding before us.

Even though we may sometimes give up on ourselves, by getting lost in someone else's shadow, we are never completely lost. For somehow, The Universe searches us out and brings us down to our knees, so that God, in His almighty goodness, can restore us to our original selves so that we too might find purpose and reason for our lives.

It is when we make the time to look within ourselves that we can get lost and find ourselves.

Planet Earth

Father forgive us for the hurt
we continually inflict
on Mother Earth
through our insensitivity
to the air that we breathe
we destroy the environment
with pollution, wars
hatred and greed
Avoiding the signs that appear
all around
in the skies, the oceans
as well as on the earth
What more will it take
for our hearts to yield
to a deeper awareness
we have laying within
To search our souls
before it's too late
for indifference may end
in witnessing
our very own
extinction...

Sitting in Judgement

If in the eyes of God all men are created equal, who then but God has the right to sit in judgement of anyone else? In light of the obvious, why then do we so often pass judgement on others as though it were our absolute right?

Self worth otherwise known as self esteem is something that we begin learning at birth. A learning that I believe can either result in the making, or the breaking of ones' spirit. This extremely important undertaking usually begins with our first teachers, our parents or whomever else undertakes the responsibility during our formative years. A covenant that often is taken far too lightly by many of us.

Unfortunately, the negative messages that are subconsciously transmitted to children, whether intentional or not, will determine the outcome and eventually the impact that it will have on their future. It is also within that particular time, that some children feel flawed and it is then that they lose sight of self worth.
It is through the negative beliefs that quite often we go through life feeling as though we do not measure up by anyone else's standards.

As life itself unfolds in its' own mysterious ways we tend to look elsewhere for validation of our self worth. It is not found within any other relationship nor does it exist in material things that one may or may not possess. Instead it is only within ourselves that we must look, for it is *we,* who hold the key to unlocking the answers that lay in wait, within us.

As we learn to solve each problem, we continue to grow, thereby, finding new strengths and power hidden within us. It is then that we are able to reconcile with our inner child. It is then that we find love of our very own.

Trusting The Lord

Be still my little heart
for I shall not give up
As long as I love
and trust
in The Lord
I know deep inside that
He works in my heart
With faith and with love
I trust in His name
for He is what He says
my Father
my Savior
my Lord

The Many Faces of Fear

It is never easy to talk about oneself, especially if it concerns one's own vulnerabilities. After all, wouldn't that be perceived as a sign of weakness by others?

Allowing for another human being to get close to us is a matter of trust. For some of us to do that is not a small undertaking.

To trust someone, is to place your life in that person's hands. How many of us can actually say that we are prepared to take the risk especially when we know it could lead to getting hurt? This thankfully is the chance we take whenever we allow anyone to get close and to know who we really are.

Somehow we learned that we do not meet the standards of our peers and further believing that, in some way or other we are flawed. Of course, the only way that we can know that is through comparison. We mirror ourselves in others to see what we are and what we are not.

This prevents us from moving forward and from making the necessary changes in our lives in order to achieve the goals we set out for ourselves. It destroys the natural instinct we have, for looking at what is around the next corner and it also stands in the way of that **Salto di Qualita or Leap of Faith**, that is crucial in our lives in order to feel our own worthiness.

When we finally learn to accept ourselves for who we are, then in turn, we can accept others for who they are.

It is only then that we are ready to embrace the knowledge that we are all one and the same with the Universe.

The Storm

A dark
stormy sky
wind and rain
pick up momentum
to thrash and beat
at the trees
the trees shudder and twist
this way and that
resistant against
the forces of the wind
a gust of wind
pushes it's way through the branches
blowing and tearing
at the leaves
hurtling them
in every direction
then finally, the calm
once more everything is still
the trees again stand tall
beneath a moonlit sky they stand
left naked
by the fury of the wind

The Wave Makers

I have long admired the idealists of this world, whom I refer to as the Wave Makers.

They are the people who believe in a cause or in someone so passionately that they are willing to go the extra mile, regardless of personal cost or consequence.

Finding out who they are is not so difficult for they are all around us. They constantly reveal themselves by their actions and teach us by example. Sometimes, they are our close acquaintances, neighbours, friends or even family members.

It would appear that each generation produces a number of these special people who, in my humble opinion, are the pioneers of change and of progress in society by giving so graciously of themselves for the good of all.

We may view these people as being different but they nonetheless are the ones who invoke change for humankind. It is through these very differences that set them apart from others, which in turn, allows them yet another route for growth, while maintaining a different way of thinking.

Unfortunately, we often repay these same individuals by judging and condemning their efforts when we accuse them of being too radical. Rather than applauding them for possessing a mind and soul of their own and a will to forge into uncharted territory.

I personally stand in awe of the Wave Makers of this world.

On A Clear Day

I felt the cold wind
blowing down on my face
as I walked by the sea
at a very slow pace
looking and seeing
as though for the first time
that which has been here
since the creation of time
never before had these eyes
taken in
the beauty and splendour
that nature is in

Two Sides of The Same Coin

Who among us is inclined to question the rules by which we were raised? Those rules learned in youth that even today can be triggered when we are pressed for a quick decision leaving us in the wake of a raft of problems, which flow from our so called "bad" judgement. Those rules which have become so ingrained in our personality that we most often choose to live and die by them rather than test them.

We might all be curious of what change can bring but questioning those rules is a completely different matter. To do so would require putting our entire belief system in jeopardy. It may even involve us having to convert to a new way of thinking.

What we have learned from these rules extremely well is how to live in fear and how to pass judgement. Judgement not only on others but also on ourselves. We have learned to view life in terms of good and bad instead of realizing that we are on this earth to quite simply experience life.

Life is not about judgement. Neither is it about condemning the actions of ourselves or of anyone else. What is our interpretation of good and bad? What scale are we using to measure it by? Are they not merely two sides of the same coin? Which side do we attempt to eliminate?

I believe that we owe it to ourselves to discover and to experience all aspects of life first hand. In doing so, we help create those unique elements that best serve our individual needs. We also learn to embrace our "good" and "bad" sides, by accepting ourselves unconditionally.

We need to do this, for it is, the blend of the good and the bad, that makes us, human.

My Home/My Haven

I have created a home for myself
from a house that had known only strife
I created a home and filled it with my essence
a home that only through
The Grace of God
turned out to be my Haven of tranquility
shared by many over the years
and most certainly by all
whom have entered my home
Many who have yearned to be accepted
While all certainly deserving of serenity in their own life
My Home, my Haven
Created in Unison with God
**that I may know peace
intimately....**

Fresh White Snow

By the light of the street lamp
you can see the snowflakes dance
Formed like prisms
in various sizes and shapes
sparkling like diamonds under the light
pure white snow
plummeting and tumbling all around
dressing the trees all in white
as well as everything else in sight
A fluffy white blanket
spread out upon the earth
offering pleasure to the beholder
and a new gift to life
Enjoyment for some, as they ski and
toboggan down the ivory slopes
New life and new beginnings for others
as life itself unfolds
Christmas with it's merriment and
celebration of our rebirth and new life
as we give honour and celebrate
the birthday of Our Lord
Jesus Christ
Fresh white snow
mirrors the
purity of life.

Fleeting

Our life I heard once said

is like a snowflake

So precious and so light

that once it touches ground

it disappears away in time

We are here for a little while

and like the snowflake that touches ground

we too shall disappear away

in time...

Acknowledgements

Sometimes a mere thank you just isn't enough. I would like to take this opportunity in dedicating **_Reflections in the Sand_** to all of those people without whom these pages might never have been written.

To my mother and father for giving me life and for having ever so generously taken care of me while sharing their love and values with me.

To my son Gaetano who means the world to me. He graced this earth with a presence through his humility, wisdom and respect and by his unconditional and unfaltering love of humanity. Always loved and remembered.

To my daughter Silvia, for her commitment and sacrifices that she has lived and her ongoing lessons that she brings of deep value and endless growth.

To my dear friend Antonietta, whom for many years has blessed me with many kindnesses, prayers, love and support. She has truly been a God sent in my life.

To my dear friend Justine, for all the love and support that we have shared, over many years, including wide spectrum talk, tears, laugher and joy, carrying us both through the many ups and downs of life.

To my son-in-law Jim, who has been an anchor of support for all of us, as he continually supports everyone with his generous and calm demeanour and with deep generosity and humility of spirit.

To my closest friends and family for their never-ending love and support.

To all those people that have passed through my life, all of whom shall forever be remembered, through the very treasures that each one of them has shared and left behind.

To my ever-loving grandsons, Andrew and Shane, along with their wives and my adorable great grand-children, Dominic and Maya, may all of your tomorrows far outweigh your yesterdays. May you always know how to love and to be loved, for love itself is truly the nectar of the Gods.

To my most kind readers, a very special thank you for having found your way to ***Reflections in the Sand***. My wish for you is that your lives be forever filled with wondrous expectations. That this journey will further lead you into finding your own true essences thus allowing you to savour each and every moment that life has to offer.

To God, for the precious gift of life and for all else that you have bestowed upon me, including the gift of self expression. With all of my heart and soul. Thank you!

Made in the USA
Middletown, DE
25 October 2023

41206217R00064